Icing Only

BY KIM KNOTT

Copyright © 2013 by Kim Knott

First Edition – October 2013

ISBN

978-1-4602-2176-1 (Paperback)
978-1-4602-2177-8 (eBook)

All rights reserved.

No part of this publication may be reproduced in any form, or by any means, electronic or mechanical, including photocopying, recording, or any information browsing, storage, or retrieval system, without permission in writing from the publisher.

Produced by:

FriesenPress
Suite 300 – 852 Fort Street
Victoria, BC, Canada V8W 1H8

www.friesenpress.com

Distributed to the trade by The Ingram Book Company

Contents

Dedication i

Chapter 1
Basic Decorator Icings 1

Basic Rolled Fondant (Sugarpaste) 2

Hints for the fondants in this booklet 4

How to use a Fondant Mat 5

Kim's Honey Almond Rolled Fondant (Sugarpaste) 10

Marshmallow Rolled Fondant (Sugarpaste) 13

Chocolate Marshmallow Fondant (Sugarpaste) 14

Small Batch Corn Syrup Rolled Fondant (Sugarpaste) 16

Amazing Butter Cream Fondant (Sugarpaste) 17

Egg White Gumpaste (Flower paste) 19

Basic Gumpaste (Flower paste) 21

Tylose Gumpaste (Flower paste) 23

Gumpaste Mix Recipe (Flower paste) 26

Chocolate Clay 29

Molding Chocolate Clay 30

White Chocolate Clay 33

Royal Icing 34

Standard Buttercream and Variations 35

Decorator Cream Cheese Icing 43

Grandma's Decorator Icing 44

Grandma's Spreadable Butter Cream 47

Meringue Powder Butter Cream 48

Petit Four Icing 50

Simple Italian Butter Cream 52

Marshmallow Butter Cream Icing 54

Boiled Water Butter Cream 57

Chapter 2
Specialty Icings 59

White Chocolate /Lemon Icing 60

Cooked Vanilla Frosting 63

Hawaiian Icing 64

Maple Cinnamon Cream Cheese Icing ... 67

Strawberry Cream Cheese Icing 68

Caramel Buttercream 71

Cooked Red Velvet Cake Frosting 72

7 Minute Frosting Simplified 75

German Chocolate Cake Icing 76

Rum and Raisin Icing/Filling 79

Tropical Swirl Icing 80

Chapter 3
Chocolate Icings and Frostings   83

Chocolate Sour Cream Icing 84

Chocolate Cream Cheese Icing 87

Swiss Chocolate Bar Icing 88

Mocha Frosting 91

Whipped Chocolate Ganache 92

White Chocolate Whip 95

Chapter 4
High Fiber Icings   97

Date, Almond Maple Icing/Filling 98

Sunflower, Apricot Icing/Filling 101

Chapter 5
Reduced Carbohydrate Icings   103

Chocolate Pudding Frosting 105

Pie Filling Frosting 106

Chapter 6
Glazes   109

Aero Chocolate Glaze 111

Summery Orange Glaze 112

Semisweet Chocolate Glaze 115

Almond Glaze 116

Yogurt Glaze 119

Appendix A 121

Appendix B 123

Acknowledgments 124

About the Author 126

About the Photographer 127

Dedication

To my Grandmother, Evelyn Gilbert, who taught me how to decorate cakes and my Mom, Suzanne Waterman, who has always inspired me to do my best and to test every recipe I put in a cookbook. Also to my husband, Stephen Knott, who has cleaned up more icing sugar in two months than anyone should have to in a year.

Cooked Vanilla Icing
holds its shape and is not too sweet.

White Chocolate Whip
is delicious and tastes good with many types of cake.

Tropical Swirl Icing
made from fruit juice and cream cheese.

Rum and Raisin Icing,
makes a perfect topping for a chocolate cupcake.

Chapter 1
Basic Decorator Icings

Basic Rolled Fondant (Sugarpaste)

1/4 cup water
4 teaspoons powdered unflavored gelatin
1/2 cup liquid glucose
1 tablespoon glycerin
1 tablespoon butter
7 cups icing sugar

1. Measure water in a heatproof bowl and add unflavored gelatin. Let stand for 3 minutes.
2. Add glucose, glycerin and butter to the bowl and then place the bowl in a large pot partially filled with hot, but not boiling, water.
3. Stir until the unflavored gelatin dissolves and the butter melts.
4. To the gelatin mixture in the heatproof bowl, add 4 cups of icing sugar. Stir together with a wooden spoon or use an electric mixer.
5. Pour mixture out onto a surface spread with icing sugar and knead in the rest of the icing sugar. (3 cups)
6. Place in an airtight container or freezer bag right away.

Notes: If the icing is sticky, add more icing sugar. This recipe makes very nice rolled fondant that looks professional. If you want to use fondant after a few days and it has hardened, soften it by microwaving it for 30 seconds.

Hints for the fondants in this booklet

Storage Times
Room temperature - 4 days
Refrigerator - 3 weeks
Freezer - 3 months

Fondant Mats
A fondant mat takes all the stress out of rolling and placing fondant on cakes. A fondant mat is two pieces of food-safe plastic that you roll the fondant between eliminating the need to dust it with icing sugar. It eliminates cracking and "elephant skin" and enables the decorator to roll out a very thin layer of the fondant. It also slows down drying as you work (See Appendix A).

How to use a Fondant Mat

1. Make the fondant into a pancake shape to roll it out.

2. Place the fondant between the two sheets of plastic.

3. Use a rolling pin to roll out the fondant to the thickness that you desire.

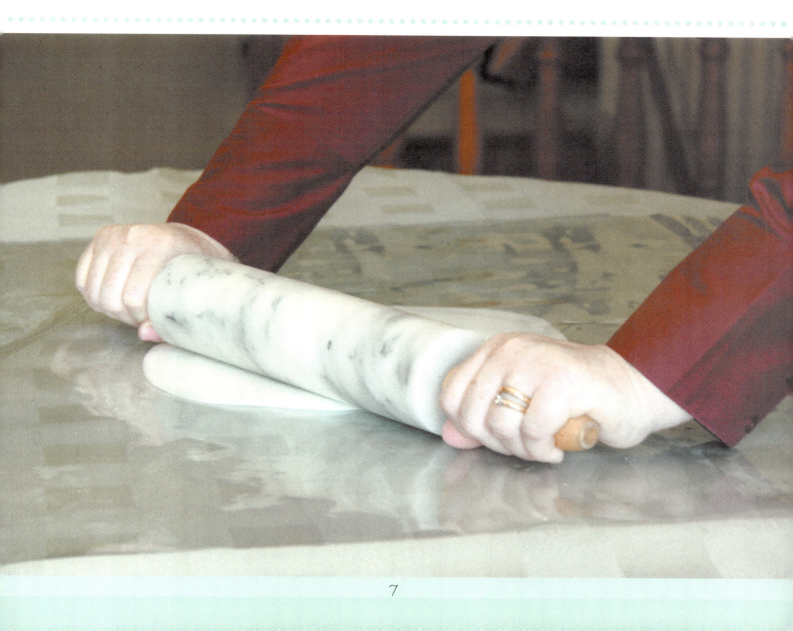

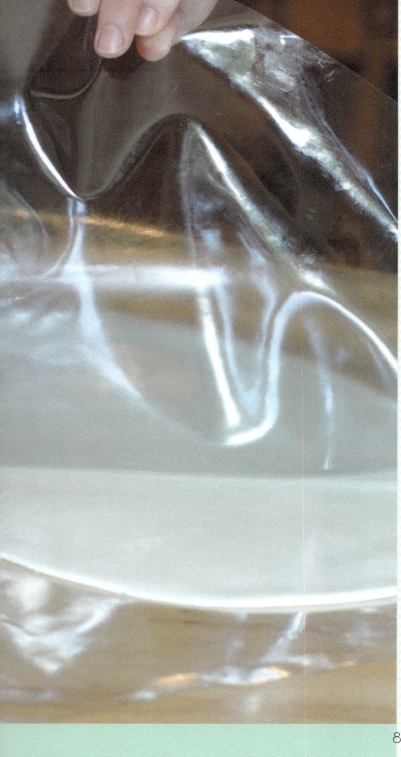

4. Take the top plastic off and then use the bottom plastic to transport your fondant to the cake. Carefully turn it over and lay it, fondant side down, over the cake and then peel off the plastic.

Kim's Honey Almond Rolled Fondant (Sugarpaste)

1/2 teaspoon almond flavoring (See Appendix B) and water to make 1/4 cup
4 teaspoons powdered unflavored gelatin
1/4 cup liquid honey
1/4 cup liquid glucose
1 tablespoon glycerin
2 tablespoons butter
8 1/2 cups icing sugar

1. Measure the flavoring in a glass liquid measuring cup and add water to make 1/4 cup, stir in unflavored gelatin and let sit for 3 minutes.
2. Pour/scrape the mixture into a heatproof bowl. Add the honey, glucose, glycerin and butter. Place the bowl into a large pot of hot, but not boiling, water. (See picture in the basic fondant recipe.) Stir until gelatin dissolves and the butter has melted.
3. In a large bowl, place 4 cups of icing sugar. Then pour warm gelatin mixture into the icing sugar and stir by hand or with a mixer.
4. Turn the mixture out onto a surface spread with icing sugar and knead the rest of the icing sugar (4 1/2 cups) into the icing.
5. Place in an airtight container or freezer bag.

Notes: Depending on the humidity and the type of icing sugar you use, you may need to add more icing sugar or a very small amount of water to bring the icing to a consistency that will allow you to roll it out. Salted or unsalted butter will work but I used salted butter to test all the recipes.

Marshmallow Rolled Fondant (Sugarpaste)

8 cups miniature marshmallows
2 tablespoons water
6 cups icing sugar
1/8 teaspoon crème de menthe oil flavoring or 1 teaspoon vanilla (See Appendix B)

1. Place marshmallows in a microwave-safe bowl with water and stir with a fork.
2. Microwave for 2 minutes, stirring after one minute.
3. Add flavoring and stir.
4. Mix 3 cups of icing sugar into the melted marshmallows, then with your hands knead in the other 3 cups of icing sugar. Store in an airtight bag or container.

Note: This rolled fondant is the easiest to make and will stay soft for 2-3 days at room temperature.

Chocolate Marshmallow Fondant (Sugarpaste)

5 cups colored miniature marshmallows (white can be substituted)
4 cups white miniature marshmallows
1/4 cup water
5 1/4 cups icing sugar
1 1/2 cups cocoa powder

1. Place marshmallows in a microwave-safe bowl, then add the water and stir with a fork.
2. Microwave for 2 minutes, stirring after one minute.
3. While the marshmallows are melting, mix together the icing sugar and cocoa powder using a fork in a medium-sized bowl.
4. Stir 3 cups of the icing sugar/cocoa mixture into the melted marshmallows. Then with your hands knead in the other 2 1/4 cups of the sugar/cocoa mixture. Store in an airtight bag or container.

Note: This fondant tends to be a little drier than the others so be sure to put some shortening on your hands before you work with it.

Small Batch Corn Syrup Rolled Fondant (Sugarpaste)

3 teaspoons unflavored gelatin
3 tablespoons boiling water
1/2 cup white corn syrup
2 tablespoons glycerin
1/2 teaspoon vanilla flavoring (See Appendix B)
6 cups icing sugar

1. In a small bowl, combine boiling water with the gelatin. Stir for two minutes.
2. Add corn syrup, glycerin and vanilla. Stir until glycerin has dissolved.
3. Add 1 cup icing sugar and stir. Then add the rest of the icing sugar and knead with your hands to form the fondant. Store in an airtight bag or container.

Note: This recipe tastes good and stays soft for days at room temperature. (Do not refrigerate this fondant.) Peppermint flavoring also works well as a flavoring.

Amazing Butter Cream Fondant (Sugarpaste)

1 cup white corn syrup
1 cup butter
1/2 teaspoon salt
1 teaspoon vanilla flavoring (See Appendix B)
8 1/2 cups icing sugar

1. Beat together the butter and white corn syrup with an electric mixer.
2. Add the salt and flavoring and beat again.
3. Add 2 cups of icing sugar and mix using an electric mixer. Then mix in the remaining icing sugar (6 1/2 cups) and knead with your hands.
4. Place in an airtight container and refrigerate for 3 hours. When cold, this fondant handles amazingly well.

Note: I called this recipe amazing because with simple ingredients it makes a remarkably workable rolled fondant. Remember, since this fondant is butter based, it will become limp at higher temperatures. This recipe may not be for the professional decorator but it is great for moms who want to use a good-tasting fondant on cupcakes for a children's birthday party.

Egg White Gumpaste (Flower paste)

2 large egg whites
8 cups icing sugar
1 1/2 teaspoons of karaya gum (See Appendix A)
1/4 cup lukewarm water (Tap water is fine. It should not feel hot to touch.)
1 tablespoon shortening (Does not go into gumpaste but is used to work with it)

1. In a medium bowl, beat egg whites with an electric mixer until frothy (about 30-40 seconds).
2. Add 2 1/2 cups icing sugar and beat until well combined.
3. Sprinkle the karaya gum on top of the mixture and then beat again for about 15 seconds. Beat in another 2 1/2 cups of icing sugar. The mixture will be dry and crumbly.
4. Add 1/4 cup lukewarm water and mix until smooth.
5. Put the final 3 cups of icing sugar in the bowl and knead in by hand. You may have to take the gumpaste out of the bowl and continue kneading.

Note: This gumpaste is a nice white color and is ready to use immediately if you use shortening on your hands when you work with it. It will be even easier to work with if you allow it to sit overnight in an airtight plastic bag or container. This gumpaste works beautifully in silicon molds. It is my favorite gumpaste recipe and dries very light and strong. Makes 2 1/2 cups of gumpaste.

Basic Gumpaste (Flower paste)

5 1/4 cups icing sugar
1 tablespoon karaya gum (See Appendix A)
1 tablespoon glucose
5 tablespoons water (4 tablespoons used first then 1 the next day)
1 tablespoon shortening (Does not go into gumpaste
but is used to work with it.)

1. Mix together 3 cups of icing sugar with the karaya gum powder in a medium bowl using a fork.
2. Combine 4 tablespoons of water and the glucose in a small bowl. Microwave on defrost for 30 seconds. Stir until the glucose has dissolved.
3. Stir the water/glucose mixture into the icing sugar mixture. This will not seem like gumpaste but instead will be a very soft icing-like mixture.
4. Put this mixture in an airtight plastic bag or container at room temperature overnight.
5. The next day, break the mixture up into 6-8 pieces and place in a microwave-safe bowl. Microwave for 30 seconds. Now mix in 1 tablespoon of water with your hands.
6. Knead in 2 1/4 cups of icing sugar. Put immediately into an airtight plastic bag or container.

Note: After kneading in the icing sugar in the last step, the gumpaste is ready to use. It always works better to put a small amount of shortening on your hands before you start working with the gumpaste because it softens it and keeps it from drying out too quickly.

Tylose Gumpaste (Flower paste)

3 teaspoons unflavored gelatin
3 tablespoons lemon juice (strained)
5 tablespoons water
1 teaspoon glucose
6 cups icing sugar
1 1/2 teaspoons Tylose or CMC powder (See Appendix A)
1 tablespoon shortening (Does not go into gumpaste
but is used to work with it.)

1. In a small microwavable bowl, combine gelatin, lemon juice, and water. Stir with a fork, then microwave for 40 seconds on high until it looks like runny honey.
2. In a medium bowl, combine icing sugar and Tylose powder and mix well with a fork. Divide this mixture into two portions.
3. Pour the gelatin/lemon juice mixture into one portion of the icing sugar/Tylose mixture. Stir with a fork.
4. In the same bowl, mix in with your hands the rest of the icing sugar/Tylose mixture.
5. Take smaller portions of the gumpaste and knead it with your hands.

Notes: Wrap the gumpaste in plastic wrap or in an airtight container and it will be ready to use in 1 hour. When using this gumpaste, put shortening on your hands to make the gumpaste more workable. It also works well in silicon molds.

Icing Tips

When making large shapes to use on top of cupcakes or cakes use gumpaste instead of fondant. It is much stronger and will hold its shape better.

Gumpaste Mix Recipe (Flower paste)

1 pound of gumpaste mix (See Appendix A)
1/4 cup water
1 1/3 cups icing sugar
1 tablespoon shortening (Does not go into gumpaste but is used to work with it.)

1. Mix the gumpaste mix in a medium bowl with 1/4 cup water and stir with a fork.
2. Add 2/3 cups icing sugar and continue mixing with a fork.
3. In the same bowl add another 2/3 cups icing sugar and knead this in with your hands.
4. Place the gumpaste in an airtight container or bag for 1 hour. Then it is ready to use.

Notes: This gumpaste will be even easier to use the next day.

Chocolate Clay

2 cups semisweet pure chocolate (See Appendix A)
2 teaspoons glycerin

1. In a microwavable bowl, heat the chocolate in the microwave on defrost for 1 minute. Stir. Then heat the chocolate for another 10 seconds and repeat until it is almost, but not quite, melted. Then let the heat of the bowl and chocolate melt the last lumps of unmelted chocolate. It is very important not to overheat the chocolate. (My total time was only 1 minute and 20 seconds in the microwave.)
2. Stir in glycerin all at once and stir with a butter knife very gently and only until the clay forms. Do not over stir.
3. Place on a plastic wrap covered plate and cover with another piece of plastic wrap. Press the clay so that it forms a 1/2 inch thick pancake on the plate and leave covered at room temperature for 1 1/2 hours.
4. Now, the clay is ready to use.

Note: I found it easiest to work with it on the day it was made. If you use shortening on your hands while shaping the clay it makes it easier. This clay works well in silicon molds and plunger cutters. (See Appendix A)

Molding Chocolate Clay

3 cups molding chocolate wafers (semisweet or milk) (See Appendix A)
5 tablespoons golden corn syrup

1. In a microwavable bowl, heat the chocolate in the microwave on defrost for 1 minute. Stir. Then heat the chocolate for another 10 seconds and repeat until it is almost but not quite melted. Then let the heat of the bowl and melted chocolate melt the last lumps of unmelted chocolate. It is very important not to overheat the chocolate. (My total time was only 1 minute and 20 seconds.) Let cool for 10 minutes.
2. Stir in golden corn syrup all at once and stir with a butter knife very gently and only until the clay forms. Do not over stir.
3. Place on a plastic wrap covered plate and cover with another piece of plastic wrap. Press the clay so that it forms a 1/2 inch thick pancake on the plate and leave covered at room temperature for 1 1/2 hours.
4. The clay is useable now, but it would be much better if left in the refrigerator overnight in an airtight container or plastic bag.

Note: When you take it out of the refrigerator, you will need to warm it up in your hands for a few minutes. Shortening on your hands will make shaping the clay easier and it works well with silicon molds and plunger cutters. (See Appendix A)

White Chocolate Clay

3 cups molding white chocolate wafers (see Appendix A)
1/2 cup glucose
1 teaspoon glycerin

1. In a microwavable bowl, heat the chocolate in the microwave on defrost for 1 minute. Stir. Then heat the chocolate for another 10 seconds and repeat until it is almost, but not quite, melted. Then let the heat of the bowl and the melted chocolate melt the last lumps of unmelted chocolate. It is very important not to overheat the chocolate. Let cool for 10 minutes.
2. Add the glucose and glycerin all at once and stir with a butter knife very gently and only until the clay forms. Do not over stir.
3. Place on a plastic wrap covered plate and cover with another piece of plastic wrap. Press the clay so that it forms a 1/2 inch thick pancake on the plate and leave covered at room temperature for 3 hours.
4. The clay is now useable, but would be much better if left in the refrigerator overnight in an airtight container or plastic bag.

Note: When you take it out of the refrigerator, you will need to warm it up in your hands for a few minutes. Shortening on your hands will make shaping the clay easier. This clay works well with silicon molds and plunger cutters. (See Appendix A)

Royal Icing

3 large egg whites
3 cups icing sugar
½ teaspoon cream of tartar (or 1 tablespoon of strained lemon juice)

1. Place all of the ingredients in a medium bowl and beat with an electric mixer on low speed until blended.
2. Turn mixer to high speed and beat for 7-10 minutes until the icing is the consistency of a stiff meringue. Icing should be thin enough to spread and thick enough to hold its shape.

Note: This icing is good for stenciling, piping lace and extension work.

Standard Buttercream and Variations

1/2 cup butter (softened)
4 cups icing sugar
5 tablespoons milk or cream
1 teaspoon vanilla flavoring (See Appendix B)

1. Beat butter with an electric mixer until creamy.
2. Add 2 cups of icing sugar. Beat until well combined.
3. Add the milk and flavoring then the other 2 cups of icing sugar. Beat until a smooth icing forms.

Variation 1 - Jelly Powder Buttercream Icing

Add 1 small (4oz) package of jelly powder and 1 extra tablespoon of milk to the butter cream icing recipe and beat until smooth. It will be slightly gritty but this will lessen if allowed to sit overnight. A good flavor is <u>Fruit Fiesta</u>. It produces a beautiful light green color. Cherry, strawberry, raspberry, peach or lime also work well and make the icing very pretty colors. This icing pipes very well.

Variation 2 - Peppermint Buttercream Icing

Instead of vanilla, add ½ teaspoon of peppermint flavoring. After step 3 add ½ cup crushed peppermint candy. If you are using oil of peppermint or crème de menthe oil flavoring decrease the amount to 2-3 drops (See Appendix A)

Variation 3 - Ginger Buttercream

Instead of vanilla, add 1 teaspoon of ginger powder and ¼ cup finely diced candied ginger.

Variation 4 - Lemon Buttercream

Instead of milk, use lemon juice and instead of vanilla add 1 teaspoon of grated lemon peel.

Variation 5 - Lemonade Buttercream

Instead of milk, add 4 tablespoons of melted lemonade concentrate and eliminate the vanilla.

Variation 6 - Orange Buttercream

Instead of milk, use orange juice and instead of vanilla add ¾ teaspoon of grated orange peel.

Variation 7 - Lime Buttercream

Instead of milk use lime juice, and instead of vanilla add 1 teaspoon of grated lime peel.

Variation 8 - Nut Buttercream

In a food processor, finely grind 1 cup of pecans, walnuts, cashews, macadamia nuts or hazelnuts. Add this to the standard butter cream recipe and beat until well combined. You can also use pre-ground pecans or almonds from the baking section of your grocery store.

Variation 9 - Maple Walnut Buttercream

Instead of vanilla, use ½ teaspoon of maple flavoring and then add ½ cup of finely chopped walnuts. (Always taste walnuts before using them because they can go rancid very easily.)

Variation 10 - Simple Chocolate Buttercream

Add 1/2 cup cocoa powder to the butter cream recipe. This icing pipes very well.

Variation 11 - Chocolate Fudge Buttercream

Add ½ cup cocoa powder and ½ cup melted chocolate chips to the butter cream recipe. Pour the melted chocolate chips in slowly while beating the icing so that the chocolate does not turn to solid in one big lump. This icing is too thick to pipe but is excellent on brownies or spread on cupcakes.

Variation 12 - Coffee Buttercream

Instead of milk, use strong coffee and add ½ teaspoon of powdered instant coffee. Do not eliminate the vanilla.

Variation 13 - Ambrosia Buttercream

Add only 3 cups of icing sugar instead of 4. Delete the milk and add ½ cup of finely chopped canned peaches and ½ cup of well-drained pineapple. Instead of vanilla, add 1/4 teaspoon of almond flavoring and 1/4 teaspoon of rum flavoring. Then to the finished butter cream, add 1/2 cup coconut.

Variation 14 - Peanut Butter Buttercream

Add ½ cup of peanut butter to the butter and mix in before adding all the other ingredients.

Variation 15 - Jelly Buttercream

Add 1/2 cup of grape, red currant or any other flavor of jelly and 1 ½ cups extra icing sugar to the finished butter cream and mix in well. The jellies will not give a strong color so you may want to add a little paste color to enhance it.

Variation 16 - Coconut Buttercream

Use coconut flavoring instead of vanilla and add ½ cup flaked coconut. Mix well.

Decorator Cream Cheese Icing

1 cup (8 oz.) cream cheese
1 tablespoon butter
3 1/2 cups icing sugar
1 tablespoon sour cream
1 teaspoon vanilla

1. Cream together the cream cheese and butter in a medium bowl.
2. Add 1 cup icing sugar and the sour cream. Beat well.
3. Add 2 1/2 cups of icing sugar and vanilla and beat well.

Note: The sour cream may be eliminated in this recipe and replaced with another tablespoon of butter. This icing goes well on carrot cake, chocolate cake or red velvet cake (see also the Cooked Red Velvet Frosting Recipe).

Grandma's Decorator Icing

3/4 cup butter
4 1/2 tablespoons cream
1 1/3 tablespoons cake flour
1 teaspoon flavoring (clear vanilla works well)
1 teaspoon glycerin
1 unbeatean egg white
3 cups icing sugar

1. In a medium mixing bowl, combine the butter, cream, flour, flavoring, glycerin and egg white. Beat with an electric mixer until well combined.
2. Add icing sugar slowly and beat well.

Notes: Makes 2 3/4 cups icing. This icing is great for cake decorating because the added flour helps it to hold its shape. The icing will be quite stiff at first but will soften as you pipe with it because of the butter content.

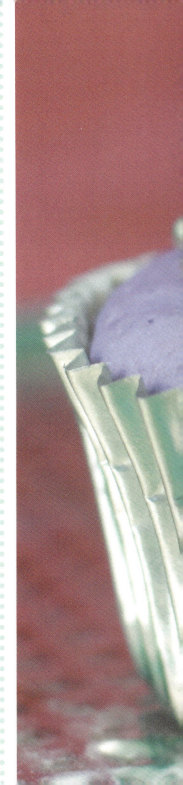

Grandma's Spreadable Butter Cream

1 cup butter
3/4 cup cake flour
1/4 teaspoon salt
2/3 cup water
2 teaspoons flavoring (clear vanilla works well)
6 cups icing sugar

1. Mix butter and flour together with an electric mixer.
2. Add salt, water and flavoring and mix with an electric mixer. Add the icing sugar gradually and continue to beat. The more you beat this the softer it will become.

Note: Makes 4 cups of icing. This is a really good tasting simple icing. This icing does not pipe well. It is designed to spread on the cake.

Meringue Powder Butter Cream

1/2 cup butter
3 1/2 cups icing sugar
6 tablespoons whipping cream
3 tablespoons meringue powder (See Appendix A)
1 teaspoon flavoring (See Appendix B)

1. Cream butter with an electric mixer, then mix in half of the icing sugar and half of the cream until well blended. Mix in the rest of the icing sugar and the rest of the cream.
2. Add the meringue powder and the flavoring and beat for 2 minutes. The icing should be fluffy and light. This icing pipes well and is more stable than basic butter cream.

Notes: To make a peppermint icing use 1 teaspoon vanilla, 1/8 teaspoon of peppermint oil and a small amount of green paste color.

Petit Four Icing

(Read though this whole recipe before starting.)

6 cups icing sugar
1/2 cup water
2 tablespoons white corn syrup
1 tablespoon glycerin
1 teaspoon flavoring - vanilla, lemon or almond (See Appendix B)

1. In a medium saucepan, combine all the ingredients and cook over low heat. It will be difficult to stir.
2. Cook the icing until there are no lumps. Then remove it from the heat.
3. Transfer to a bowl and cover with plastic wrap until you are ready to use the icing.
4. Cut your cake into small pieces and lightly spread them with a butter cream icing. Put them on a tray in the freezer for 2 hours.
5. Take them out of the freezer. Put a spoonful of the petit four icing on the top of each small cake. With a knife, gently push it to the sides of the cake. Now wait. The icing will flow over the sides slowly. You may have to help seal the corners or add more icing.

Note: If you do not have a lot of patience this may not be a good recipe for you.
When the icing has flowed down the sides, trim the edge where the icing meets the plate then freeze them again. This prevents the icing from continuing to flow down. They will only need about 15 minutes to defrost.

Simple Italian Butter Cream

4 egg whites
3/4 cup white granulated sugar
1/4 cup white corn syrup
1 1/2 cups butter at room temperature (cut up into 1 inch cubes)
1 teaspoon flavoring - vanilla, lemon, orange or almond (See Appendix B)

1. Find a medium bowl that fits into a slightly larger bowl. Put about 2 cups of cold water from the tap into the larger bowl. In the medium bowl, beat the egg whites with an electric mixer until soft peaks form. Set aside.
2. In a small saucepan heat the sugar and white corn syrup until it comes to a boil, stirring the entire time with a heatproof spatula or wooden spoon. Remove from the heat immediately and pour the liquid slowly into the egg whites while beating with the electric mixer. Beat for 2 minutes.
3. Set the bowl into the larger one that has the cold water in the bottom. Let cool for 3 minutes or until the bowl is the same temperature as your hand.
4. Beat in one cube of butter at a time. Then beat the icing until it changes consistency. This will take 2-3 minutes. You can now add coloring and flavoring.
5. If you need to keep this icing for a few days put it in the refrigerator and then beat it again just before you want to pipe it.

Note: Cooling the egg whites and syrup in the water bath eliminates the need for beating for 10 minutes. If you don't have a large mixer this is a great energy saver.

Marshmallow Butter Cream Icing

1 cup butter (room temperature)
1 (7oz) jar marshmallow cream
3 cups icing sugar
1 teaspoon vanilla
1 teaspoon coconut flavoring

1. In a medium bowl, mix together the butter and marshmallow cream until well combined.
2. Add the icing sugar and beat for 1 minute. Add the vanilla and coconut flavoring and mix again.

Note: This icing is light and fluffy and tastes great.

Boiled Water Butter Cream

1 cup butter
5 cups icing sugar
1 tablespoon vanilla
3/4 cup sugar
1/4 teaspoon salt
1/2 cup boiling water
1/4 cup meringue powder

1. In a medium bowl beat together butter, icing sugar and vanilla.
2. In another bowl, stir together sugar, salt, boiling water and meringue powder.
3. Pour boiling water mixture over butter/icing sugar mixture and beat until smooth.
4. Refrigerate for 20 minutes.

Note: This icing will be too soft to pipe well but spreads very nicely. Using a food processor to make this icing also works well.

Chapter 2
Specialty Icings

White Chocolate /Lemon Icing

1 cup cream cheese
1/2 cup butter
3/4 cup icing sugar
1 cup white chocolate wafers - melted (measure after melting)
1/4 cup freshly squeezed lemon juice
1/2 teaspoon lemon rind (finely grated)
1/8 teaspoon yellow paste food coloring (See Appendix A)

1. Melt the white chocolate in a small glass bowl in the microwave approximately 1 minute on defrost and then for 10 seconds as many times as needed to melt. Let it cool.
2. Beat the cream cheese, butter and icing sugar in a bowl until smooth.
3. Gradually beat in the cooled white chocolate, lemon juice, rind and food coloring.

Notes: This icing would be good on a white or lemon cake. It was a favorite of my taste testers.

Cooked Vanilla Frosting

1 cup milk
5 tablespoons flour
1 cup butter
1 cup icing sugar
1 teaspoon vanilla

1. Cook the milk and flour over low heat stirring constantly with a whisk until it forms a paste. Let cool for at least 15 minutes.
2. In another bowl, mix together the butter, icing sugar and vanilla with an electric mixer.
3. Add the flour and milk mixture to the butter and icing sugar mixture. Beat for 5 minutes until light and fluffy.

Note: This icing is a nice consistency for spreading on a cake but not at all sweet. It makes 2 cups of icing.

Hawaiian Icing

1/4 cup sugar
2/3 cup evaporated milk
1/3 cup canned pineapple juice
3 egg yolks
2 cups finely shredded sweetened coconut
1/2 cup canned crushed pineapple (drained)

1. Combine sugar, evaporated milk, pineapple juice and egg yolks in a small saucepan and cook over a medium heat, stirring with whisk until mixture boils for 30 seconds. This will take a few minutes and you must be careful not to let it burn.
2. Let cool and add coconut and crushed pineapple.

Notes: This would also make a good filling for white, yellow or coconut cakes.

Maple Cinnamon Cream Cheese Icing

1/3 cup butter
1 cup cream cheese
3 cups icing sugar
2 tablespoons maple syrup
1/8 teaspoon maple flavoring (See Appendix B)
1/2 teaspoon cinnamon

1. Mix together the butter and cream cheese with an electric mixer until well combined.
2. Add icing sugar, maple syrup, flavoring and cinnamon and mix well.

Notes: This icing tastes great on a yellow cake. It was a big hit with the taste testers.

Strawberry Cream Cheese Icing

1 cup of butter (right out of the refrigerator)
1 cup cream cheese (right out of the refrigerator)
5 cups icing sugar
3 tablespoons finely diced fresh strawberries or raspberries
1/2 teaspoon vanilla

1. In a medium bowl, beat the butter and cream cheese together using an electric mixer until well combined. Beat in the icing sugar.
2. Add the berries and vanilla and continue beating until icing changes to a pretty pink color. Do not over beat.
3. If you want a stiffer icing, cover and refrigerate for 1½ hours.

Notes: This icing works well on chocolate cupcakes or a strawberry cake. You may have to add more icing sugar to the icing depending on the water content of the strawberries. You also may have to add a small amount of pink paste color if your strawberries do not give enough color. Keep this icing refrigerated and remember it is butter-based and will become soft in a hot room. It can be frozen for 1 month in a plastic bag or airtight container. This is a great tasting icing and well worth the effort.

Caramel Buttercream

1/2 cup premade caramel (melted) (See Appendix A)
4 tablespoons cream (divided)
1/2 cup butter
4 cups icing sugar
1 teaspoon vanilla
1/2 teaspoon salt

1. In a microwavable bowl, melt premade caramel for 45 seconds on high. Add 2 tablespoons of cream and microwave again for 45 seconds.
2. Stir the hot caramel and cream together until they form a sauce. This will take a minute of stirring. Let cool.
3. In a medium bowl, beat butter, icing sugar, vanilla and salt until it is combined and crumbly. Slowly add the caramel sauce and then the other 2 tablespoons of cream and beat well.

Note: This makes a firm icing that is perfect for piping. For more caramel flavor, you can make more of the caramel sauce (Step 1) and drizzle it over your finished icing. This icing goes well with yellow or chocolate cake.

Cooked Red Velvet Cake Frosting

1 cup milk
4 tablespoons cornstarch
1 cup cream cheese
1 1/2 cups icing sugar
1 teaspoon vanilla

1. Cook the milk and cornstarch over low heat stirring constantly with a whisk until it forms a paste. Let cool for at least 15 minutes.
2. In another bowl, mix together the cream cheese, icing sugar and vanilla with an electric mixer.
3. Add the cornstarch and milk mixture to the cream cheese and icing sugar mixture. Beat for 1-2 minutes until light and fluffy.

Note: This is the ultimate red velvet cake icing. It is too soft to pipe but spreads well.

7 Minute Frosting Simplified

3 egg whites
1/4 teaspoon cream of tartar
1/2 cup corn syrup
3 tablespoons water
1 cup sugar
1/8 teaspoon salt
1 teaspoon vanilla

1. In a medium bowl, that is free from any grease, beat the egg whites until frothy. Add the cream of tartar and beat until peaks form. Leave this with the mixer ready to beat again in a few minutes.
2. In a medium saucepan, combine the corn syrup, water and sugar. Stir over low to medium heat until bubbles form around the edge of the pot. Set a timer for 1 minute. Stir with a wooden spoon or heat-resistant spatula. Remove immediately from the heat.
3. Slowly pour the hot syrup over the egg whites while beating the mixture.
4. Beat for at least 3 minutes or until stiff peaks form.

German Chocolate Cake Icing

1 cup sugar
1 cup evaporated milk
1/2 cup butter
3 eggs (beaten)
2 cups shredded coconut
1 cup pecans (chopped)
1 teaspoon of vanilla

1. Whisk together the sugar, evaporated milk, butter and eggs. Cook on medium heat until the mixture begins to boil. Remove from heat. You will need to watch and stir this the whole time.
2. Mix in the coconut, pecans and vanilla. Let cool.

Note: This traditionally goes on a German chocolate cake but it is good on yellow cakes and other chocolate cakes, too.

Rum and Raisin Icing/Filling

1 cup brown sugar
2 tablespoons cornstarch
1/4 teaspoon salt
3/4 cup milk
2 tablespoons white corn syrup
1 teaspoon vanilla
1/2 teaspoon rum flavoring (see Appendix B)
1 1/2 cups coconut (shredded)
1 cup pecans (chopped)
1 1/2 cups raisins

1. Heat the brown sugar, cornstarch, salt, milk, and corn syrup in a small saucepan, using medium heat, until the mixture boils.
2. Add the vanilla, rum flavoring, shredded coconut, pecans and raisins and stir.

Note: This makes 2 3/4 cups of icing. It would be good on a Kentucky Butter Cake, yellow cake or dark chocolate cake.

Tropical Swirl Icing

Fruit Gel
2 cups of tropical juice (guava, pineapple or tropical mix)
1/2 cup sugar
1/4 cup cornstarch
3 tablespoons water
1 drop of red food coloring (optional)

Marshmallow Icing
1 cup cream cheese
1/3 cup sugar
1 teaspoon vanilla or ½ teaspoon coconut flavoring
1 cup Cool Whip

1. <u>Fruit Gel</u> - In a small saucepan mix the tropical juice and sugar together and bring to a boil.
2. In a small bowl, mix together the cornstarch and water until it forms a paste.
3. Gradually add the cornstarch mixture to the hot fruit juice while stirring. Continue heating until the mixture thickens.
4. <u>Marshmallow Cream</u> - Cream the cream cheese and sugar together.

5. Add the vanilla. Then fold in the Cool Whip.

6. Either swirl the two icings together on a cake or put a line of gel up inside a decorator bag and fill it with the marshmallow icing to get a swirled piping effect.

Chapter 3
Chocolate Icings and Frostings

Chocolate Sour Cream Icing

1 cup semisweet chocolate chips
1/2 cup sour cream
1/4 teaspoon salt
2 1/2 cups icing sugar
1 teaspoon vanilla

1. In a small bowl, melt chocolate chips in the microwave. (Approximately 1 minute on defrost, then for 10 seconds as many times as needed to melt.) Set aside.

2. In a medium bowl, blend sour cream, salt, icing sugar and vanilla. Add melted chocolate slowly and beat until well blended.

Note: This makes 2 cups of a simple, good tasting icing. It would be good on any chocolate or marble cake and is great for piping.

Chocolate Cream Cheese Icing

2/3 cup cream cheese spread (soft in a tub)
2 tablespoons brown sugar
5 tablespoons whipping cream
1 teaspoon vanilla
3 - 1 oz squares unsweetened chocolate (melted)
1/3 cup cocoa powder
2 cups icing sugar

1. In a microwavable bowl, melt the chocolate squares. (Approximately 1 minute on defrost then for 10 seconds as many times as needed to melt.) Let cool.
2. In a medium mixing bowl, using an electric mixer, mix together cream cheese, brown sugar, whipping cream, vanilla, and cocoa powder.
3. Add the icing sugar and blend well.
4. Now slowly add the melted chocolate and blend well.

Note: This makes 2 1/2 cups of icing. This icing is good on any chocolate, maple or white cake. It pipes very well.

Swiss Chocolate Bar Icing

2 - 100 gram Swiss chocolate bars
2/3 cup butter
2 cups icing sugar
2 tablespoons cream or milk

1. In a microwavable bowl, melt the chocolate in the microwave. (Approximately 1 minute on defrost then for 10 seconds as many times as needed to melt.) Set aside to cool.
2. Cream butter then add icing sugar and cream or milk. Beat until smooth.
3. Add melted chocolate slowly. Beat until fluffy. As this icing cools it becomes very thick. If you need to soften it for cake decorating, then microwave it on defrost for 20 to 30 seconds.

Notes: If you use a chocolate bar with nuts use a big decorator tip (like 1M size decorator tip) so that it will not clog. This makes 2 cups of icing and is good on any chocolate, white or marble cake. This icing would be good on blackcurrant-jam-filled cupcakes.

Mocha Frosting

1/2 cup soft tub margarine (or butter)
3 cups icing sugar
2 tablespoons strong coffee
1/4 teaspoon salt
1/4 cup chocolate ice cream topping
3 tablespoons cocoa
1 tablespoon vanilla extract
1/2 teaspoon powdered instant coffee

1. In a medium bowl, using an electric mixer on medium speed, cream together the margarine and sugar until combined and crumb like.
2. Add the remaining ingredients. Beat for 3 minutes.

Notes: Makes 2 cups of icing. This icing would be good on a chocolate, spice, white or angel food cake.

Whipped Chocolate Ganache

2 1/2 cups chocolate or white melting wafers
1 cup whipping cream (35% milk fat)
1/2 teaspoon flavoring or 1/8 teaspoon oil flavoring (optional) (Appendix B)

1. Melt the chocolate in a small saucepan until just melted.
2. Stir in whipping cream and stir with a spatula until smooth.
3. Add flavoring and stir to mix in.
4. Transfer to a mixing bowl. Let cool for 5 minutes then beat with an electric mixer until the ganache changes to a light brown color. This is perfect for piping on chocolate cupcakes.

Note: If you eliminate whipping the ganache, it can be used as a glaze on top of a cake or cupcake. A good combination is half milk chocolate wafers and half dark chocolate wafers. Nuts can also be mixed in.

White Chocolate Whip

¾ cup white chocolate waffers
2 cups whipping cream (35% whipping milk fat)

1. Place chocolate in a bowl.
2. In a small saucepan, heat 1 cup of whipping cream until bubbles form.
3. Pour over chocolate and stir until blended.
4. Whisk in an additional 1 cup of whipping cream
5. Cover and refrigerate for 4 hours.
6. Whip mixture with an electric mixer on high until stiff peaks form.

Note: This icing will pipe quite well for about ½ hour after it is made and it will keep for 1 day in the refrigerator.

Chapter 4
High Fiber Icings

Date, Almond Maple Icing/Filling

1 cup dates
1 cup water
1 cup ground almonds
4 1/2 cups icing sugar
1/2 teaspoon maple flavoring (See Appendix B)

1. Place the dates and water in small saucepan and cook for 10 minutes or until the dates are very soft.
2. Let cool, then place them in a food processor and add the rest of the ingredients. Process until the icing is smooth.

Notes: This is good on spice, date or white cakes. My youngest daughter said this was the best icing she ever tasted.

Sunflower, Apricot Icing/Filling

3 cups dried apricot
1 cup water
1 cup unsalted roasted sunflowers seeds
1 cup peach or orange juice
1 1/2 cups icing sugar
1/4 teaspoon grand marnier oil flavoring (See Appendix A)
1/4 teaspoon vanilla

1. Place apricots and water in a small saucepan and cook on medium heat until water boils. Cook for 2 minutes then let cool.
2. Drain stewed apricots then place in a food processor. Add sunflower seeds and orange juice and blend until smooth.
3. Add icing sugar and the two flavorings and blend until smooth.

Note: This may be used as an icing or filling with a white or spice cake.

Chapter 5
Reduced Carbohydrate Icings

Chocolate Pudding Frosting

1 small package (1.4 oz) sugar-free Jell-O instant chocolate pudding
1 cup milk
1 envelope Dream Whip

1. In a medium bowl, combine all three ingredients and beat with an electric mixer until smooth.

Note: This frosting is great on carbohydrate reduced muffins or plain cake.

Pie Filling Frosting

1/4 cup sugar
2 tablespoons cornstarch
2 cups milk
2 egg yolks (beaten)
1 teaspoon vanilla
1 cup sugar reduced pie filling (lemon, cherry, or strawberry-rhubarb)

1. In a saucepan, measure in the sugar, cornstarch and milk. Cook on medium heat until mixture comes to a boil stirring with a whisk the whole time. This takes 4-5 minutes.
2. Take 1/2 cup of the hot pudding mixture and mix it in the eggs. Stir. Add the egg mixture slowly to the hot pudding, stirring with a whisk the whole time.
3. While still warm, add the vanilla and the pie filling.

Note: This frosting is great on carbohydrate reduced muffins or plain cake.

Chapter 6
Glazes

Aero Chocolate Glaze

4 - 42 gram Aero Chocolate Bars (milk chocolate with bubbles)
1 cup sour cream
2 tablespoons granulated white sugar

1. In a small saucepan, at a low temperature, melt all the ingredients together.
2. Spoon onto the top of cake or cupcakes.

Summery Orange Glaze

1 cup orange juice
3/4 cup sugar
2 tablespoons lemon juice
2 tablespoons cold water
2 tablespoons cornstarch
1 teaspoon almond flavoring (see Appendix B)
1/8 teaspoon lemon peel (finely grated)

1. Combine orange juice, sugar and lemon juice in a small saucepan and heat until boiling.
2. In a small bowl mix together water and cornstarch and stir until there are no lumps.
3. Whisk the cornstarch mixture into the orange juice mixture and cook on medium low heat until it just starts to boil.
4. Remove from the heat and add the almond flavoring and lemon peel.

Semisweet Chocolate Glaze

1/4 cup cream or milk
1 tablespoon white corn syrup
1/2 cup semisweet chocolate chips or semisweet wafers

1. In a small microwavable bowl, melt together the cream, corn syrup and chocolate in the microwave. (Approximately 1 minute on defrost then for 10 seconds as many times as it needs to melt.)
2. Stir with a whisk or a fork until the mixture is well combined. Do not be discouraged if it does not form a sauce immediately. It will take a minute or two of stirring.

Note: The quality of this glaze is determined by the quality of the chocolate you use.

Almond Glaze

2 tablespoons butter
1/2 cup white chocolate wafers
6 tablespoons milk or cream
1 cup icing sugar
1/2 cup ground almonds
1/8 teaspoon vanilla
1/8 teaspoon almond flavoring (See Appendix B)

1. In a small to medium microwavable bowl, melt together the butter, white chocolate and cream in the microwave. (Approximately 1 minute on defrost then for 10 seconds as many times as needed to melt.)
2. Mix in icing sugar, almonds, vanilla and almond flavoring.

Pecan Variation: Substitute ground pecans for the ground almonds and use 1/4 teaspoon of vanilla instead of 1/8 teaspoon. Eliminate the almond flavoring.

Note: This would be good on a chocolate, coconut or almond cake.

Yogurt Glaze

2/3 cup icing sugar
2 tablespoons flavored yogurt (raspberry, strawberry, or peach)
paste color (optional) (Appendix A)

1. In a small bowl, mix together the icing sugar with the flavored yogurt then add paste color if desired.
2. Spread on cupcakes or cake.

Appendix A

J. WILTON DISTRIBUTORS
EDMONTON, ALBERTA
j-wilton.com

The following products can be ordered from J. Wilton Distributors.
CARAMEL - Premade ready to use.
CHOCOLATE, MOLDING - milk, semisweet and white
CHOCOLATE, PURE
CLEAR VANILLA
CMC - Tylose (Sodium Carboxymethylcellulose)
GLUCOSE (liquid)

GLYCERIN

GUMPASTE MIX - comes in 1 pound packages

FONDANT MAT - The Mat

FONDEX - A good tasting, easy to use, premade rolled fondant

KARAYA GUM - also known as GUM TEX

MERINGUE POWDER

OIL FLAVORINGS - 25 flavors available (almond, raspberry, rum, etc.)

PASTE COLORS - ideal for coloring icing so that the consistency does not change.

PLUNGER CUTTERS - flowers, butterflies, snowflakes

SILICON MOLDS - leaves, flowers, animals

WHITE-WHITE Icing Color - Whitens or lightens icing

Appendix B

Tips

1. Flavorings are different from oil flavorings. When a flavoring is used, it is an alcohol- based product from a grocery store. When an oil flavoring is used it is a special product usually only found in specialty stores. The quantity used is very different. Oil flavorings are much more concentrated and therefore you use a much smaller amount for the same flavor intensity.
2. If you want a whiter icing use clear vanilla instead of regular vanilla.
3. There are only two places shortening is used in this book. It is used on your fingers to make gumpaste and chocolate clay more pliable. In all the other recipes butter was substituted for shortening because I don't think shortening is a good fat to consume. It is, however, almost always necessary to use when working with gumpaste because it doesn't go rancid as quickly as butter.

Acknowledgments

I decided to write a recipe book as a tribute to my Grandmother, Evelyn Gilbert. Grandma started her cake decorating career in her fifties and went on to become an excellent cake decorator and gumpaste artist. My mother, Sue Waterman, has owned J. Wilton Distributors since 1976. J. Wilton Distributors is a cake decorating retail/wholesale distributor of cake and chocolate making supplies with online access to thousands of items. It is located in Edmonton, AB. (j-wilton.com) This business started as a retail store where my Grandmother taught cake decorating and gumpaste classes for many years. I decided to take the little book she made for her cake decorating classes, expand it, modernize it and sell it as a cookbook. I would like to thank Kim Quisquis for all the typing she did to help us out and my husband, Stephen, who did a great job of helping me proofread it. I would also like to thank my photographer, Ramona Wiebe, for her beautiful pictures that make my cake decorating look good. I love to cook and I think I have developed some recipes that are great for icing cakes, easy to make and taste good. I do not own a big mixer so all of these recipes have been made with a small electric mixer and with Canadian icing sugar that contains cornstarch. Two dollars of each printed book sold is going to go to my favorite charity, Children's Camps International (ccicamps.com). I hope you have as much fun with these recipes as I did writing the cookbook. Kim Knott

About the Author

Kim Knott lives in Manitoba, Canada and grew up with a mother who owns a cake decorating supply company and a grandmother who was a gifted cake decorator and gumpaste artist. Kim has a foods and nutrition degree from the University of Alberta and loves to cook, garden and sew.

Look on Facebook http://www.facebook.com/IcingOnly for more information about this cookbook.

About the Photographer

Ramona Weibe is a wife and mother of four children. She can often be found enjoying life behind the lens while cheering her family on at mountain bike races or taking pictures while hiking in a nearby valley. She enjoys crafting, sewing, prairie sunsets and camping. She is also involved in fundraisers to support projects in Ethiopia and, together with her youngest daughter, enjoys making Ethiopian food. She loves to bake and create gluten-free meals. She has tried some of these delicious icing recipes for her children's birthday parties. Some of her projects can be found at willowdalewhimsy.blogspot.com.

CPSIA information can be obtained
at www.ICGtesting.com
Printed in the USA
LVIW02n1218031213
363587LV00001B/4